Hyena
Who's Laughing?

by Natalie Lunis

Consultant:
Kay E. Holekamp, Ph.D.
Department of Zoology
Program in Ecology, Evolutionary Biology, and Behavior
Michigan State University

BEARPORT
PUBLISHING

NEW YORK, NEW YORK

4/12

Credits

Cover, © Beverly Joubert/National Geographic/Getty Images and Steffen Foerster Photography/Shutterstock; TOC, © Eric Gevaert/Shutterstock; 4–5, © Anup Shah/Minden Pictures; 6, © Animals Animals/SuperStock; 7T, © Minden Pictures/SuperStock; 7B, © Marka/SuperStock; 8, © NHPA/SuperStock; 9, © Image Source/SuperStock; 10–11, © Biosphoto/Michel Bureau; 12T, © Minden Pictures/SuperStock; 12M, © Anup Shah/npl/Minden Pictures; 12B, © NHPA/SuperStock; 13, © Minden Pictures/SuperStock; 14, © Minden Pictures/SuperStock; 15, © Science Faction/SuperStock; 16T, © Minden Pictures/SuperStock; 16B, © Biosphoto/Michel & Christine Denis-Huot; 17, © Joe McDonald/DRK Photo; 18T, © Minden Pictures/SuperStock; 18B, © Minden Pictures/SuperStock; 19, © Imagebroker/Photolibrary; 20, © age fotostock/SuperStock; 21, © Gallo Images/Sondag/Liza van Deventer/Alamy; 22, © Daniel Alvarez/Shutterstock; 23TL, © Minden Pictures/SuperStock; 23TM, © F1 Online/SuperStock; 23TR, © Marka/SuperStock; 23BL, © Biosphoto/Tony Crocetta; 23BM, © Anup Shah/npl/Minden Pictures; 23BR, © Uryadnikov Sergey/Shutterstock.

Publisher: Kenn Goin
Editorial Director: Adam Siegel
Creative Director: Spencer Brinker
Cover Design: Dawn Beard Creative and Kim Jones
Photo Researcher: Picture Perfect Professionals, LLC

Library of Congress Cataloging-in-Publication Data

Lunis, Natalie.
  Hyena : who's laughing? / by Natalie Lunis.
      p. cm. — (Animal loudmouths)
  Includes bibliographical references and index.
  ISBN-13: 978-1-61772-278-3 (library binding)
  ISBN-10: 1-61772-278-2 (library binding)
  1. Hyenas—Juvenile literature. I. Title.
  QL737.C24L86 2012
  599.74'3—dc22

                            2011012737

For more information, write to Bearport Publishing Company, Inc., 45 West 21st Street, Suite 3B, New York, New York 10010. Printed in the United States of America in North Mankato, Minnesota.

073011
042711CGE

10 9 8 7 6 5 4 3 2 1

Contents

A Strange Laugh

A hyena runs across a grassy **plain** in eastern Africa.

In its mouth, it is carrying an antelope that it has killed.

Another, stronger hyena chases it to try to grab the food away.

As the hyena with the antelope keeps running, it makes a series of strange, **high-pitched** noises.

The sounds are like a loud giggle.

Antelopes are deer-like animals. Hyenas hunt and eat them.

antelope

Not So Funny

The fast-running hyena is not making *hee-hah-hee* sounds because something is funny.

Instead, its giggle is a kind of nervous laughter.

Hyenas often laugh when they are worried or upset—for example, when another hyena tries to steal their food.

The laugh is one of many sounds that the animals make when they are around one another.

Hyenas look like a kind of wild dog, but they are not related to wolves, foxes, coyotes, or any other kind of wild dog. Instead, they are closely related to mongooses.

mongoose

"Laughing" Hyenas

There are four different species, or kinds, of hyenas.

Only one of them has a loud laugh, however.

It is known as the spotted hyena because of the spots on its fur.

People also call it the laughing hyena because of the unusual sounds it makes.

All four kinds of hyenas live in Africa. One kind, called the striped hyena, also lives in parts of Asia.

striped hyena

Spotted Hyenas in the Wild

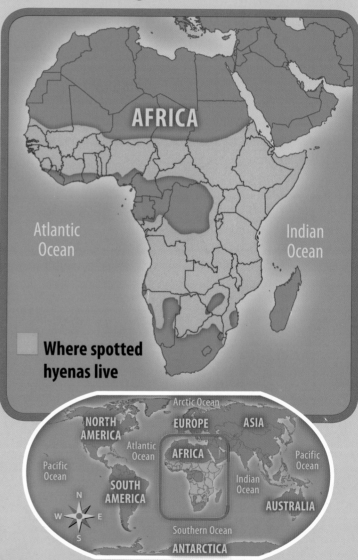

AFRICA

Atlantic Ocean

Indian Ocean

Where spotted hyenas live

Arctic Ocean

NORTH AMERICA

EUROPE

ASIA

Atlantic Ocean

AFRICA

Pacific Ocean

Pacific Ocean

Indian Ocean

SOUTH AMERICA

AUSTRALIA

Southern Ocean

ANTARCTICA

spotted hyena

9

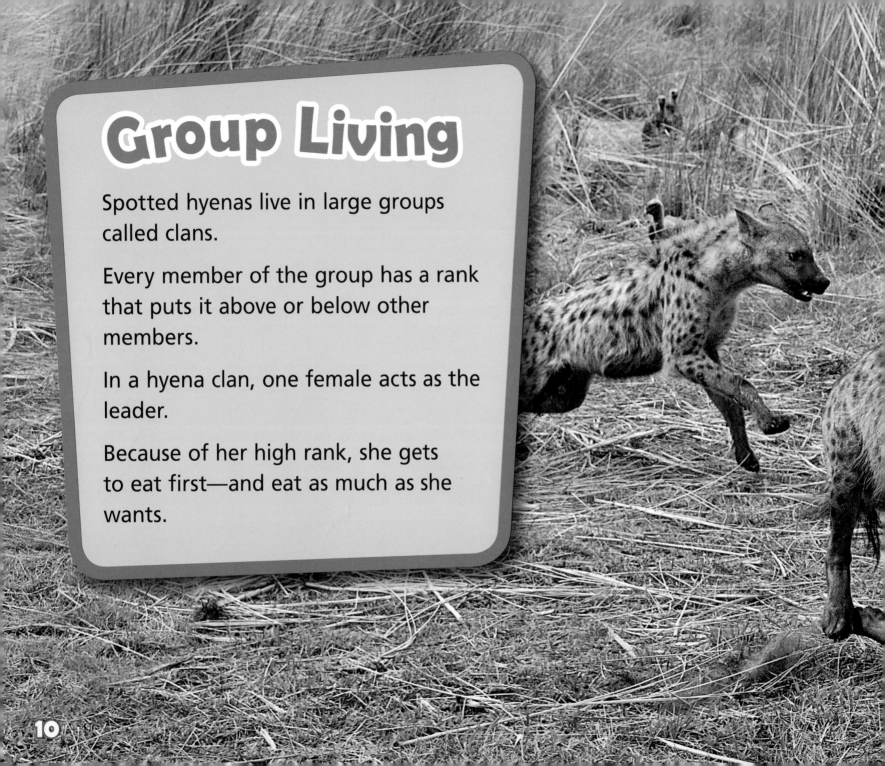

Group Living

Spotted hyenas live in large groups called clans.

Every member of the group has a rank that puts it above or below other members.

In a hyena clan, one female acts as the leader.

Because of her high rank, she gets to eat first—and eat as much as she wants.

hyena clan

There are up to 90 hyenas in a clan.

Hunting and Whooping

Spotted hyenas are hunters.

They kill and eat small animals such as birds and lizards, as well as larger animals such as antelopes and zebras.

Most of the time hyenas hunt on their own.

Sometimes, however, hyenas hunt with other members of their clan to catch zebras, giraffes, wildebeests, and other large **prey**.

flamingo

antelope

wildebeest

When hyenas spread out to search for food, they send messages by making loud whooping sounds. For example, sometimes hyenas whoop when they find hyenas from other clans in their **territory**. The whoops call clan members to come over to help chase the other hyenas away.

Looking for Leftovers

Spotted hyenas do not only hunt for food—they are also scavengers.

That means they eat the bodies of dead animals, including ones that have been left behind by lions, cheetahs, or other meat-eaters.

Often, the hyenas eat parts of a dead animal that other animals cannot.

They have powerful jaws and strong teeth that help them crunch and chew up bones.

They can even eat a dead animal's fur.

strong teeth

Hyenas are the most common large meat-eater on the African grasslands. There are many more of them than lions or cheetahs.

Noisy Meals

Sometimes hyenas are able to chase one or more lions away while the big cats are still eating.

Then the spotted animals start their own noisy meal.

Higher-ranking hyenas eat first, often growling at one another between bites.

Lower-ranking hyenas giggle and whine as they wait their turn—or try to sneak in and grab a chunk of food.

hyenas chasing away lions

When a hyena is trying to steal food away from lions, it whoops. The call tells other clan members to come quickly and help.

Keeping Cubs Safe

Baby hyenas are called cubs.

They spend the first few months of their lives in **dens** that are dug out of the ground.

There, they are safe from enemies such as lions or hyenas from other clans.

Little by little, the young hyenas start exploring the outside world.

Usually they stay near their mother.

If a cub wanders out of sight, it may whoop to call its mother—or a mother hyena might whoop to call her cub back.

cub

den

Hyenas are **mammals**. Like all mammal babies, a hyena cub at first gets food by drinking milk from its mother's body. As it grows up, it starts eating the same foods as adult hyenas.

cub drinking milk

19

Listening Closely

Spotted hyenas usually stay far away from people.

How, then, do scientists know about the many sounds they make?

One group of researchers studies the animals in a surprising place—Berkeley, California.

In 1985, the scientists brought 20 hyenas from eastern Africa to live in a large fenced area in Northern California.

Today, there are almost twice as many hyenas, because some have given birth to cubs.

Together, the noisy, intelligent animals give the people around them plenty of chances to listen and learn.

Scientists based in Berkeley work with scientists who study hyenas in the wilds of Africa. In the years to come, they hope to learn more about the meaning of hyena sounds in both settings.

Sound Check

Scientists who study spotted hyenas have learned that the animals make at least 14 different kinds of sounds. The most famous is the laugh—also called the giggle—which signals that a hyena is excited, nervous, or upset. Here are some of the other sounds that spotted hyenas make:

Sound	Purpose or Meaning
whoop	the hyena is calling other hyenas to come over
groan	the hyena is greeting another hyena; a mother hyena is telling her cubs to come out of their den
whine	the hyena is begging other hyenas to let it eat
growl	the hyena is telling another animal to back off

Glossary

dens (DENZ) hidden places, often underground, where animals can rest and hide from enemies

high-pitched (HYE-PICHT) sharp and almost squeaky

mammals (MAM-uhlz) warm-blooded animals that have a backbone, have hair or fur on their skin, and drink their mother's milk as babies

plain (PLAYN) a large, flat area of land

prey (PRAY) an animal that is hunted and eaten by other animals

territory (TER-uh-*tor*-ee) an area of land that belongs to and is defended by an animal or a group of animals

Index

Read More

Grucella, Ethan. *Hyenas (Animals That Live in the Grasslands).* New York: Gareth Stevens (2011).

Pearl, Norman. *Hyenas: Fierce Hunters (Powerful Predators).* New York: Rosen (2009).

Richardson, Adele. *Hyenas: Hunters and Scavengers (The Wild World of Animals).* Mankato, MN: Capstone (2002).

Learn More Online

To learn more about hyenas, visit
www.bearportpublishing.com/AnimalLoudmouths

About the Author

Natalie Lunis has written many science and nature books for children. She lives in the Hudson River Valley, just north of New York City.